Working Parent
by
Paula Johanson

While every precaution has been taken in the preparation of this book, the publisher assumes no responsibility for errors or omissions, or for damages resulting from the use of the information contained herein.

WORKING PARENT

First edition. July 25, 2024.

Copyright © 2024 Paula Johanson.

ISBN: 978-1989966280

Written by Paula Johanson.

For all those with stories of their own to tell.

Introduction

Parents are thinking and talking more about the process of raising a child these days. When the "child" is twins, and home shifts from a downtown industrial park on the harbour in Victoria, British Columbia, to a tiny farmhouse fifty miles north of Edmonton, Alberta, there is plenty to think and talk about. I've been writing some of those thoughts for my friends and for Canadian magazines.

Gardening with kids changes from growing a pet squash to hoeing a four acre market garden that gets bigger every year. Long drives mean that the fine art of keeping the children peaceful is almost the only art form my husband and I have time for. Indoor games take on new importance when the West Coast rain has been pouring for three weeks or the thermometer hits -45°C in a Prairie winter.

Raising twins on a modest income in a modern world is best faced and described with good humour. The stories collected here have been read by parents and writers, looking for a smile and something true about parenting. Pre-natal classes don't teach everything, though Lamaze breathing did help me some on the morning the babies cried, the kettle whistled, and the phone and the doorbell rang all at the same time.

My friends had their children on the installment plan – one at a time, whether or not they could afford them. I had twins, both up front with no money down.

I should have danced all night. I haven't since. Still, I never sleep the night through, between one of my family kicking off the blankets or the other rolling thunk! against the wall, or another beginning to snore like a Johnson outboard motor.

No, the third restless sleeper isn't another kid, that's my husband, Bernie. Their sleeping habits all affected me one fall when we were sleeping in the guest room in my parents' home. We hadn't all slept in one room since the day Bernie and I brought the twins home from the hospital. That day we put our newborns in two matching laundry baskets (when you have twins, you learn how to make substitutes for $50 bassinettes) at the foot of our bed. Every time one of the twins exhaled, we leapt out of bed, panicking. The next night they went in their own room, with both doors open and I heard every squeak or cry. Bernie slept through that night, which I assume is why he approved of the new arrangement.

Sharing the guest room at my parents' house didn't meet up with his approval or mine, but we made the best of it for two months. In between living in an old Victorian duplex and moving to a tiny Prairie farmhouse, those two months were a time without paid work, after working in a community centre once the twins were three years old, and before working on our small farm. Though I didn't have work to keep me busy, I kept busy at my typewriter, from habit learned when the twins were small and later kept up during four years on the farm.

Some of the notes I made during those two months became the following observations. Other parts of this book were written in between growing seasons on the farm in Alberta. (Note: Nothing gets written during the growing season. At that time, if I'm not seeding, weeding or picking, I'm selling vegetables. Write stories? Hah! I'm lucky if there's time to bathe!) And the rest was written during two winters we ran away from Prairie blizzards back to Victoria to enjoy snowdrops in January and cherry blossoms in February.

Some of these stories appeared in *Island Parent* magazine and *Winnipeg Parent Newsmagazine* before being collected here. Most of them were read aloud at poetry readings in The Cove, a community centre which has always made time and space for families and their stories. I made a lot of friends there, and also while writing the stories for my first book, *No Parent Is An Island*. More than anything else in *Working Parent*, I want to share that welcome feeling other parents have given me.

Don't look here for a self-help manual. But if you like to share your disasters and daymakers with friends, this book has some stories about how fun and scary it was while my toddlers grew to school age. It also shows some of the changes in me, as my Christmas Wish List ranges from a state-of-the-art computer to a decent chocolate chip cookie recipe.

The Working Parent's Chant

Tonight I do the laundry, loads of dirty clothes and whites
    The rumble of the wringer washer punctuates my nights
    Then I wash the kitchen floor of all the mud my kids have tracked
    I'm a Working Parent and my patience is taxed.

THIS MORNING I LEARNED porridge burns like napalm when it spills
    On my hands which will be blistered when I dig potato hills.
    Will I have to chase the coyote that our duck flock does attract?
    I'm a Working Parent and my patience is taxed.

MY PARTNER TAKES HIS turns with me for who's on Kid Patrol
    And who will Roto-till the garden for our weed control.
    The kids go swinging from the trees and digging holes out back
    I'm a Working Parent and my patience is taxed.

THE SCHOOL MY KIDS attend has cutbacks – and a lot of cheek!
    Librarians were laid off so I sorted books this week.
    Got asked to volunteer when program funding was axed...
    I'm a Working Parent and my patience is taxed.

THE KIDS GOT INTO BASEBALL, swimming, skateboards and their bikes
    Do you know what it costs to buy a size four pair of Nikes?

Still, picnics on the beach are fun and we make barefoot tracks
I'm a Working Parent and my patience is taxed.

MY FRIENDS AND FAMILY babysit, lend cars and work and more;
    I'll lend a hand to pay them back till we're all ninety-four.
    At least I'm not in debt like folks whose credit cards are maxed!
    I'm a Working Parent and my patience is taxed.

AT DINNER TIME I CALL my crew, but sometimes it gets cold
    (Computer programs are more fun than veggie casserole)
    When hunger strikes them all I'll get my word processor back!
    I'm a Working Parent and my patience is taxed.

SOME PEOPLE TELL ME what I need so I don't slob around
    Is to put on nylons and a dress for real jobs downtown.
    Looking after kids is real work! It's plain and simple fact.
    I'm a Working Parent and my patience is taxed.

SO TONIGHT I DO THE laundry and then I'll wash the floor
    I'll make long-distance calls and hear my guy tell jokes and more
    The outside world? Well, CBC AM keeps me on track.
    I'm a Working Parent and my patience is taxed.

Do You See Anybody Else Here Who Is Naked?

How to go out with kids: open the door and go outside.

Oh, are shoes important? Or winter coats? Okay, start again...

How to go out with kids: bundle them up. Find socks and shoes. Pants and shirts may be necessary, and sweaters or coats if the weather warrants. It got so I kept a bag by the door ready to go out, with two diapers, two big cotton kerchiefs (they make dandy bibs, sunhats, neck scarfs, or diapers in a pinch), fruit leather, a "drinkin' box of fruit juice", my wallet, keys, a stamped envelope and a pen so I could write to friends asking if they knew why I had kids.

One grand expedition with the twins began rather well. We were off to Ryan's birthday party, well bundled up as it was January. Our old car, called Underfoot (because something always was), had enough seatbelts for Laurie and her boy Evan as well as the twins and I. After I parked downtown, we paraded in our parkas to the theatre where we met the rest of the birthday party, to see a play based on *The Hobbit*. The four adults in our party were at least as excited as the six children.

When we reached our seats, there was still some time before the curtain would rise. But I was prepared, with extra supplies in my bag of goodies, to keep the kids from getting restless.

"I'm hot, Mama," complained three-year-old Lila.

"Take your coat off, sweetie, and you too, Ben," I told the kids. Ryan and Evan and the other kids followed suit, and we mothers took the coats and sat in the row behind the kids.

As the kids started to squirm, I asked: "Does anybody want jelly babies?" There was a half-pound of them in my bag.

"Me please!" chorused all the kids and two of the moms.

"I'm still hot, Mama," Lila complained again.

"You can take off your sweater, Lily," I said while rootling through my bag. I came up with the jelly babies and passed some to everybody, moving along the row of cupped hands till I came to... Lila... who had taken off her sweater... and her t-shirt... and was sitting in her panties, pulling her sweat pants off over her boots. "Lila Marie!" I whispered. "Put your clothes back on!"

"But I'm really hot, Mama," she said blandly.

I groped for something to say that wouldn't traumatize her like screaming NAKEDNESS IS DIRTY. "Do you see anybody else here who is naked?" I whispered. "This isn't a place to be naked in. People wear clothes here." It didn't get results. I looked around quickly, and saw my friends convulsed in silent laughter. No help from them.

After an eternal few seconds, Lila held up her cupped hands. "Can I have some?"

Inspiration struck for the second time. "I can't give you any jelly babies till you put your shirt and pants on," I said. "Everybody eating jelly babies is wearing clothes."

"But I don't wanna get hot again," Lila insisted.

By this time *I* was getting hot under the collar. "So don't put your sweater and boots on," I said calmly, and held the bag of fruit candy where she could see it. She cheerfully squirmed back into her t-shirt and pants and got a handful of jelly babies. Meanwhile I was giving the dirtiest looks I could manage placidly at my friends, who were nearly blue from silent laughter. "Why didn't you tell me she was undressing?" I hissed, suppressing my own grin.

"Oh, you took care of it just fine," Kris chortled. "Do you see anybody ELSE here who is naked?" she quoted, and held her ribs. The curtain rose mercifully soon. Years later, Kris can still make me laugh by saying it again.

How to go out with kids: bring a sense of humour along with the jelly babies. At least.

Out of the mouths of babes

In any school yard or daycare, the voices of children can be heard talking, laughing, shouting, crying... and occasionally cursing a blue streak. I know four-year-olds who use words I had never even heard till I was eighteen. And it wasn't that I led a sheltered childhood, or that children nowadays all lead rough-and-tumble lives. As near as I can tell, many people's habits are changing to include more obscenities and curses in everyday talk.

This does not mean only that people are calling one another hateful names more often these days – though that does seem to be happening, and it leads to exchanges of curses and "Same to you!" between drivers who would never think of saying "Good morning!" if that rotten so-and-so had just yielded and let their car into the turn lane. No, it means also that foul words get used more familiarly to describe feelings, without being directed at cursing any one else in particular.

The mother of my two godsons has been known to use foul language. But I've paid attention, and noticed that even as she says, "Oh, (blank)! I've got such a (blank)ing headache, I'm going to (blank)!" – she never calls her kids names. She will turn to the boy tugging on her sleeve for the umpteenth time while she cooks supper, and say "Go away for a while. I'm so (blank)ing angry, I've got a (blank)ing headache. Give me a break, honey." So while her boys do hear her swearing, they have never been called a foul name, or put down with rough talk. And strangely enough, the boys rarely use these harsh words. Apparently they don't get as (blank)ing angry as often.

Curses and obscenities have been heard and/or said by everyone these days. This seems to be true for some adults and some children. Foul language is less common among my family and friends... except in certain circumstances which expand our children's vocabulary. So far, the twins still nod sagely when I remind them that "some words are for when Daddy drops the hammer on his foot."

But even before we moved to the land of breaking tractors and loud cursing, our daughter looked down into her dinner one evening and quietly said a word I'd last heard from the driver of a Mack truck when he was cut off by a red sports car.

Bernie and I looked at each other and at our four-year-old angel. Bernie kept chewing, I swallowed first and lost. "What was that, dear?"

"Billy called Sam that at daycare today. What is that?"

"It's something some people say when they're angry. It isn't nice." Somehow I kept a straight face while Bernie tried earnestly to keep chewing without choking. In another moment he'd get me laughing, too, and I wouldn't be as silent. "We don't call people names like that."

"Oh." She thought for a minute. "What a silly sound." She said it again, contemplating the shape and sound of an ugly word. And she went back to eating dinner. We may have a sound poet on our hands, the next in the Canadian tradition of Doug Barbour and Steven Scobie, exploring the sound of words.

Indoor Games

Our kids enjoy riding bikes or digging holes in the garden, but sometimes rainy days or cold winter weather keep them indoors. After a few rounds of their current favourite games, such as, "Those are *my* crayons!" and, "Quit sneaking around turning off all the lights!" the twins turn to me for amusement. Since I no longer have any crayons and am content to sit in the dark, drinking tea and looking out the rainy window, they don't find me very amusing. Before long, they want me to actually *do* something interesting for them.

This was easier when they were toddlers, even when they wanted attention while dinner was cooking. Each child was handed a pot or metal mixing bowl and a wooden spoon. They knew what to do next. In this way, my husband and I became aware of the importance of earplugs for parents who are not yet hearing impaired. Our uninitiated dinner guests took a little time adjusting to the "wall of sound" in the kitchen.

"Listen!" Bernie urged one guest. "He just played the opening drum riff from David Bowies's *Young Americans*! That's my boy!"

The guest nodded, unconvinced. "I can help you wash and dry the pans before putting them away," he offered. Obviously he was unclear on the concept. The battered pans were just plain put back in the cupboard – but we always washed them before and after cooking, I hastened to explain. He said he believed me, but he ate mostly bread and butter at dinner that night. Entertaining friends at dinner with children around can be difficult.

Entertaining the children after dinner can be difficult with or without guests. I tried baking with the twins' help, but they stirred cookie dough at curtain-splattering speeds; and whenever I reached for ingredients they'd reach into the bowl for a taste. To stop them pulling yeasty handfuls from my dinged-up bread bowl, one day I gave each of them their own piece of bread dough to knead. Success! They were too intrigued by the texture to think of eating it, and before long they were shaping snakes and Ninja Turtles on pans to rise and bake with the regular loaves.

The crooked, swollen shapes that were so satisfying then, especially eaten hot with butter, don't get the same response now. The kids are older, and want to do things well. They want real success, not just Daddy's "Wow!" In short, they want to win at games now, and if possible, beat someone else doing it.

So this winter we tried playing Crokinole, Snakes & Ladders, SORRY and Monopoly, and brought out the hockey game my brother and I played with as kids.

Have you ever realized how many games need someone to lose in order for someone to win and the game be finished? Once we re-invented sibling rivalry, Bernie and I discovered how it is that parents can find it in their hearts to put little kids into snow gear and send them into a blizzard to run around for a while. It warmed up enough one day to rain instead of snow, and I let the kids play in a downpour. When they came in for supper, their coats were stiff with icicles but they hadn't argued even once.

This made it clear that indoor games involve competition as much as they involve a certain amount of parental attention. I tried instead to look on games as tools of socialization and lessons in co-operation, but it came down to the basics: some gotta win, some gotta lose.

"... Goodtime Charlie's got the blues," I hummed during a fierce, cut-throat game of Crokinole, which is a sort of table-top curling in the round. The kids didn't really have the coordination to play it well, or the ability to plan ahead well for a wickedly good game of Monopoly. (Besides, we didn't have the new Canadian version, with foreign corporations and colourful political figures.) Snakes and Ladders was more their speed anyway, although Lila could get lost in the middle of the board and end up going backwards. And as far as I was concerned, a table top hockey game needed to have penalties just like real hockey. It needed a referee, after all.

Finally, it seemed that our family made a game suit us all, with strategy that invited co-operation, winning with grace and losing with dignity. Nuclear Combat SORRY (with house rules: cheering allowed, but no tears, and alliances betrayed at will) worked well for us until Bernie consulted with the kids about how to stack the deck, "To keep Mommy from winning the very next round."

Oh, he laughed and shuffled the cards again; but when I turned up the jinxed card anyway, he knew there would be no indoor games for us that night when the kids were asleep.

In the interests of marital harmony we later tried other card and ball games with cousins, but it was their Oma (paternal grandmother) who taught the twins to play Hand & Foot Canasta. I didn't think they could hold eleven cards, or the second hand everyone was dealt. But sometimes kids can do more than parents know. Team playing helped, and it kept everyone busy and getting along until the weather cleared up and we played ball.

You Drive Me Crazy

The colours changed in the sky as I watched the sun dipping behind a hill in an alfalfa hayfield. The car roof echoed like a drum to an interior wail that rose and fell intermittently. I heard a motor start up, about a quarter mile away. A young man in his late teens had left the nearest farmhouse and was now riding a "quad" (one of those four-wheeled motorcycles) along the driveway and down the gravel road in our direction. I rolled down my window as he pulled up beside the car.

"Having any trouble?" he asked. "Need a hand?"

"No, thanks. We're just taking a break," I told him. "The kids were fighting." The back seat was perfectly silent now, and neither kid so much as breathed heavily. The guy looked puzzled, so I asked, "Did you ever drive with kids kicking up a fuss?"

He blushed a little. "No, but my parents did."

"Then you know how hard it is to settle fights in a moving car. I pull over for a while." He nodded then. I added. "We won't be long here. Thanks for seeing if we needed help." He smiled, turned the quad around and headed back up the road. As he zoomed away, I turned to look at my kids in the back seat. "Are you ready to go now?"

"Yes, Mom," they said soberly, in unison.

Thus ended one of the more difficult times we've ever had in the family car. Some folk can handle more noise than I can, others travel happily singing endless choruses of "Old McDonald." When I learned to drive, I learned to stop the car if the kids were having any sort of trouble, like tantrums or biting their own tongues. It sure beats swerving across the centre line!

EVERY DRIVER HAS SAFETY habits to deal with passengers or road conditions. Before my family moved to the farm, one afternoon my friend Kris called me at work, during that rarest of Victoria experiences, a daytime snowfall. "Hi there," came her brassy voice over the phone. "Have you looked outside lately? It looks just like Trail, where I grew up." She went on, "I'm just calling my friends who drive to see if they know how to get home safely in all this white stuff."

"Yeah, I think so. Avoid hills, change speed or direction with caution, steer into the skid – if the back end slides left, steer left to straighten out the car," I said, feeling something like a game show contestant. "And if there's a reason for going over twenty miles an hour in town, I don't know it."

"You'll make it," Kris said, chuckling confidently. "Got lots more people to check on before they leave work," she added before hanging up.

Sometimes I wish I had her confidence on the road, especially on the back roads by the farm. After three winters, I now have the skill to drive at 80 km/h over frozen roads, while yahoos in red pick-ups are passing me at 110 km/h. Since I am a cautious driver, people behind me must get frustrated. One night a driver was so incensed that I kept to the speed limit in a downpour, that he found it necessary to pass me, crossing a double yellow line, downhill on a blind curve. I do hope he knew about the ravine before coming upon it so suddenly.

Bernie calls drivers like that "evolution in action." If only they didn't take out so many of the rest of us while finding out about the survival of the fittest... Still, reckless drivers aren't something I can change. I can only improve my own skills, and carry safety equipment: blanket, first aid kit, shovel, snack food, fishing rod, notebooks. Yeah, yeah – what do you think kids, a fisherman and a writer would need if something came up?

THE MOST IMPORTANT factor in my kids' safety on the road is me, not only driving carefully around gravel trucks, but listening to them making various noises with their toys or snacks. When they were four, I gave them each a peppermint one morning on the way to day care. It was an ideal treat, I thought.

Peppermint doesn't melt like chocolate all over the car seats, nor does it come out of the mouths like suckers, which I had come to despise after The Duel of the Fuzzy Lollipops. The twins had forehead bruises after that battle and I had a migraine headache.

It was only because I was listening to the twins as I drove that I heard the tiny sound when Lila choked on her peppermint. The next several things happened almost in the same instant: my glance flicked up to the rear-view mirror where I saw Lila's eyes start to go round and her hands begin to flail, as I hit the brakes and noted no other vehicle was immediately behind us. I was out of my seat belt and heading into the back seat as Lila's little body was slammed against the seat belt on her booster seat. The belt gave her an improvised Heimlich manoeuvre that popped the peppermint out of her throat with a 'whuff' of breath. Relief!

Both kids were startled, and immediately spat out their candies for me. They needed a moment's comfort. Behind us came another vehicle, and I think that driver could see me crawling back into the front seat, for there was only a short beep instead of an obnoxious long honk. There was enough going on to make any driver crazy.

Fishing With Kids – Bait Optional

Bernie is the fisherman. I just like the outdoors and the twins like being outside exploring Wild Nature. It used to be that Bernie would go off for a while during our hikes and fish by himself. When we all got rods, we began to fish together. The kids liked this better, but to my surprise Bernie found it frustrating.

No, he didn't suggest that "fishing with kids" meant pitching these noisy beings into the water for fishbait. Many times we all ended up swimming anyway instead of fishing, after the kids scared all the fish away with the drumming of their footsteps and their ear-piercing screeches whenever they found frogs, or pretty stones.

"Look, Dad! A stick with a forked end!" Ben beat the water to foam with his stick. Bernie sighed and put away his tackle.

After a few sessions fishing the Sturgeon River, I realized that Bernie was setting up the tackle for all four rods. This took time. We couldn't stay long before making the hour-long drive to get the six-year-old twins and their ravenous appetites home for dinner. Between setting up tackle and showing the kids how to cast, Bernie didn't get much time to put his own lures in the water. So I learned how to set up rods, too, and made sure Bernie got to walk upriver to his own quiet pool under the willows for at least a little while.

Our fishing gear consists not only of rods, reels and tackle, but a snack, juice and a nature book to identify all the wildlife the kids find. We also keep a blanket in the car because summer evenings can be chilly for kids in shorts. I keep a nifty little lure in my pocket for when the twins get antsy and their father is around a bend in the river, casting into a deep green pool. This lure isn't tackle, it's an Annikin pocket-sized book, available at many bookstores across Canada. The Robert Munsch titles, especially if smeared with a little peanut butter, are sure to hook the kids' attention for a few minutes.

We have to be a bit flexible in our approach to fishing expeditions. If Ben yells "Garter snake! Wow! I just saw a real garter snake!" Lila will drop the lures and both kids will kick over Daddy's tackle box in their hurry to chase the snake. Later, while sorting lures and hooks, there's an opportunity for telling the tall tale about fishing with a tree frog lure and catching a snake... our kids know that one by heart. "And the snake was rubbin' up against his ankle," Lila finishes the story, "with *two* tree frogs inniz mouth!"

That tall tale came to mind when Ben saw preserved frogs on sale, and talked his dad into trying them. The frog drifted in the Sturgeon River's slow current, something like a live frog, and coaxed a northern pike out from under a sunken log. They could see it checking out the frog and touch it before darting away. Our son almost screamed, and Bernie gasped, "Wow! Most people *never* get to see a fish rise to a lure," he told Ben.

Our kids still talk about the day Ben first actually landed a fish. Ben talks about how hard the fish pulled on the line, and how good he felt walking over to his grandfather's house to fry the fish for breakfast. Lila talks about how she has never caught a fish of her very own, and sheds jealous tears. This has taught our family to say "*WE* caught a fish," and to share the glory as we share the scrambling along river banks. No one catches a fish all by his or herself, unless the rod and reel is handmade or the fine art of trout tickling is used. The people who keep the river clean, build the roads or re-stock lakes – don't they help, too?

Many children are learning about the environment and ecological concerns in school, but it is out in the wide world where they can see the truth of these matters. The contrast between clean and fouled places becomes obvious even to kids when they spend time outdoors. Love for natural places is learned by experience, not by slogans and marketing.

It doesn't take a lot of expensive tackle or specialized equipment to go fishing as a family. A cheap rubber worm lure can be a shared treat – especially the ones Lila talked her dad into buying. "The sparkly ones, Dad! They look like My Little Pony toys! This one is *soooo* neat. Can I keep it?" She did. In her pocket. Where I found it on laundry day. A sparkly pink maggoty thingummy with a wriggly tail. Oooogh.

Lures aside, we find the biggest investment is time, shared with the twins and their friends. It's worth it, for now and the future. These kids will grow up to become workers and owners of clean businesses, or at least voters for future Environment Ministers. Right now, we're trying to give them rivers and bays they can care for, always.

Just a Homemaker?

It isn't fashionable any more to say "I'm just a homemaker." Lately it seems that stay-at-home parents are either supposed to be chief executive officers of our own corporations, taking a year or ten off to have children, or else we proudly wear aprons that read "Nothin' says lovin' like somethin' from the oven." Well, my apron says "Every Mother is a Working Mother." But even if I'm comfortable working at home and being a homemaker, not everyone I deal with is comfortable with the idea.

For one, there's my mother-in-law. She loves her grandchildren and would never dream of telling me to let the little ones come home to an empty house after school... yet every month for years she thoughtfully cuts out Position Vacant ads (for which I am over- or under-qualified) and considerately tells me what I need is a job. Reminding her that I have three jobs (market gardening with my husband, writing articles and reviews for several newspapers and magazines, and raising the kids) doesn't help; apparently real work means commuting fifty miles to the city for a large paycheck. It is nice to know she thinks I deserve a big paycheck!

For another, there's the editor of a monthly tabloid newspaper who bought one of my stories. When he said, "It must be nice to be a homemaker instead of working," and smiled patronizingly, I saw red and wrote him a blistering note outlining some of the community services I have done while a homemaker and also the editor of a monthly tabloid. Later when we met at the Book Fair on Family Day, he was business-like and polite. I didn't bother telling him I'd sold my Christmas List to Island Parent Magazine; who cares if he calls it real work?

But the people I've met who most of all don't know what to think about homemakers are police. I've had wonderful conversations with officers in Neighbourhood "Cop Shops" who treat me like a professional writer, teacher or recreation programmer who came to discuss important community issues. Then the words "No, I can't stay for a cup of coffee, I have to get the kids from the babysitter" pass my lips. Poof! Suddenly what I say doesn't matter so much, and gets answered with little words in short sentences.

Maybe it is hard for these people to imagine homemakers as anyone other than Beaver Cleaver's Mom in her spotless house with a pot roast in the oven, or perhaps the opposite stereotype of a soap-opera addict whose family eats Kraft Dinner out of the box. Maybe it is up to me and my husband, who has taken his turn as home-parent and homemaker, to show the people we know that homemakers can be as interesting and intelligent as working people anywhere.

I did put "Homemaker" on my resume when I applied to teach this winter. The superintendant of schools gave me a look of fierce pride and said, "I know how homemakers plan and organize and juggle children's needs. I was a homemaker for years." And she didn't say "just a homemaker," either!

The Creatures from the Old Movie Festival

For Quality Time, for nostalgia and a sense of comfort, give me an old science fiction movie any time.

In these days of television and satellite channels, when 70% of Canadian homes have more than one television set and a VCR, families tend not to go out to the movies often. A video rental store is more likely to be near home, than is a movie theatre. Popcorn is cheaper at home, videotapes can be put on "pause" and when the kids go to bed, the adults can watch their own videos.

Drive-ins were nearly as good for families as videos when I was a kid, but there aren't many drive-in theatres any more. And the movies that have G and PG ratings these days! Kids can end up watching murder, mayhem and sexism at $5 or more a seat. It's easy to understand why some families opt for videos and satellite channels.

Many homes are lit by the blue flicker of a TV, where children are happily watching murder, mayhem and sexism at home – for $2 a video rental, or on satellite by paying some exorbitant rate. I would never spend that kind of money on something as trivial as mere television. Instead, we take our kids over to their grandparents' houses, to watch TV with their VCR and satellite dish. Only once in a while, I swear.

I've become aware that because of this occasional style of TV watching, our twins are watching different shows from the standard juvenile fare of violent cartoons and game shows. Kids are generally not shown old monster Sci-Fi movies these days. Sharing old classics like *The Creature from the Black Lagoon* may bring warm moments of family togetherness, but it also led to hundreds (I'm not joking, hundreds) of drawings by our son and blank confusion on the part of his first-grade teacher.

Suddenly, every drawing and writing assignment Ben did had monsters on it. Or graveyards. Or spaceships. The teacher couldn't figure this out. What did *he* know? It was his first year on the job, and here's a six-year-old asking how to spell Gamora and Medusa. Does Godzilla have teeth or breathe fire? This wasn't covered in his Language Arts classes at University!

The teacher asked Bernie and I to come for an interview. The desk was covered with Ben's pencil drawings of graveyards, shambling monsters and spaceships. "I don't know what all this means," the teacher admitted apologetically. "I was taught during my Educational Psychology course that if a kid draws graveyards and frightening monsters, he might be afraid of death or worried because of a funeral in the family."

Bernie peered at one drawing. "Oh, no, this is a scene from an old movie we watched last weekend. *Plan Nine from Outer Space* has a graveyard scene with cheap cardboard tombstones that wobbled. Bela Lugosi died just after they started filming, so they did the rest of his role using an out-of-work dentist who was a foot taller and looked nothing like him." Bernie laughed. "That's the vampire Ben drew with the cape in front of his face."

"And the U.F.O.'s?" the teacher asked, still puzzled.

"That one's the spaceship from *Forbidden Planet*," I said. "We watched that the other day. This other one's from the magazine that published my story last year."

"Your... story?" He sounded like he didn't believe it.

"I write science fiction stories," I explained. "Some of them have been published in magazines here and in Vancouver. We read lots of SF books. I review books for the newspaper, too. Did you see my review in the Books Section this week?"

Of course he hadn't seen it. Poor man, he was more confused than ever. "And the monsters? Sometimes kids are acting out the scary things they're afraid of, I read in my textbook."

We inspected the brightly-coloured dinosaur drawings, and the sketches of dancing, toothy monsters. "My happy tyrannosaur," I read off one drawing. "These monsters are smiling because they're strong and powerful. When Ben's feet were healing, we encouraged him to imagine himself as strong and powerful."

"Did you ever read Maurice Sendak's book *Where the Wild Things Are?*" Bernie asked the teacher. "The boy in that story visits wild things with teeth and claws, but they don't hurt him because he says *no*. Ben and Lila love that book."

Some of it began to sink in. "Well, he's not drawing his own funeral, that's for sure. And his monsters aren't hurting any people, they are just big and strong," the teacher admitted. "Could he be writing and drawing about what you do for a living?"

It was probably that, so for next "Show and Tell" day Ben went to school with a bag full of magazines and clippings from the newspaper. "These ones have my mom's stories in them. These are articles my mom wrote for the newspaper. When she sold this one, we went to McDonald's!"

When we picked the kids up at school, the teacher was smiling. "I can't get the song your son was singing out of my head," he said, as Ben came by, singing a tune from R.E.M.'s current album. "It's the end of the world as we know it, and I feel fine." "It's a brave new world, isn't it?" said the teacher. At the end of the school year, he went back to University for more courses. He knew he hadn't learned enough yet.

At the library, our son takes out books on mythology and old movies, pouring over the pictures and spelling out the words. If he sees a familiar monster, he cheers. If a monster movie is on video or satellite, sometimes he sees it with his sister while his Dad and I make monster snacks – peanut butter on rice cakes, with faces made of raisins, or jam on Stoned Wheat Thins, with faces made of nuts. I figure this has got to be better for him than playing Freddie Krueger and the Boogeyman with kids from school.

The positive results of all this monster mania are many: long conversations between kids and parents discussing the how-tos of make-up and special effects, the kids writing their distant uncles and aunts ("Today I saw Godzilla!") and if nothing else, the grandparents finally have some idea what to give the kids for birthday presents.

Home Office

My home office is a place that sees a lot of traffic. My working day may find me working on a novel, a book review or an article for *Island Parent* magazine while my second-hand ADAM computer's printer taps away. One or both of the kids will be in looking for felt pens, erasers and paper. Bernie will need envelopes and the address files for the heap of correspondence he's been typing in the kitchen.

Other elements in the busy home office include my brother-in-law dropping it to ask when we'll need some of his cover cloth for our row crops in the market garden, and perhaps a phone call will come through from a car wash that services only black cars, just as I am waiting for my editor to let me know how many books he wants reviewed this month.

Keeping all this in mind, I figure the most important requirement for someone with a home office is the ability to stop work, take care of the interruptions, and *get back to work*. This is more important than investing in a new computer, state-of-the-art software or even earplugs. Why? Because the office is at home, where interruptions occur whether work-related or not. How many times do carpet cleaners call a fifth-floor office? And relatives and neighbours don't often say, "I thought I'd come by since you were just sitting there all alone," when there's a receptionist and a boss to get past first.

It's an occupational hazard of the home office that the worker may end up receiving appliance repair technicians as well as couriers with new work assignments. Being home at lunch may tempt me to go out and pull garden weeds for half an hour, but it's up to me to get back to work. And as I am at home, when kids are sick, it falls to me to put work aside at least until the parent working 9-to-5 gets home.

It's hard to explain to a kid who got used to Mommy daubing his chicken pox with calamine lotion – *every twenty minutes for a week*! – that he's better now, and he should play Lego or read while Mommy's working. It's even harder to explain why staring at a monitor screen while words scroll back and forth, and making occasional corrections, is actually called working. It's particularly hard if, while the computer is printing, Mommy nods off, tired from all those late nights working after the Chicken Pox Kid falls asleep.

With all the worry these days about work-related injuries, how come nobody has written a Workers' Compensation pamphlet about typing with wrinkled fingers? After the Chicken Pox Kid (Mark II) needs four baths a day to soothe her poor, itching tummy and back, Mommy has fingers like pink raisins.

My friend, the would-be fantasy writer, has an IBM compatible system which out-perfoms anything available pre-1988 for love or money – and no complete manuscripts to send to market. I wrote three novels and a dozen stories on the typewriter which saw me through University, before buying my second-hand ADAM and becoming a freelance writer. Sometimes I even work one-handed while hugging kids or sorting market garden seeds in my busy home office. Fancy equipment is awfully tempting, though. After reading the review of notebook computers in *The Computer Paper*, I knew I wanted the portable qualities of a notebook.

So I bought one. Spiral bound, five subject dividers and lined paper. I can even take it to the pool and write fiction or reviews while my kids take swimming lessons. It works. So do I.

Home Computer

We were under a little pressure to buy a computer for the kids. First off, the schools all have computers now, and even in grade two our kids knew that "the smart kids get more out of Computer Time." I learned as a freelance writer how useful computers can be, not only for the usual repetitive office work, but for self-employed people in all fields of work. And my godsons' mother began pushing computers and Nintendo as the best way to keep kids busy and happy that she ever found.

Of course, at that time she lived in downtown Vancouver where it's an urban adventure to walk kids to the Library, school or park. Did she let my godsons play alone outside? Not on your life. But my kids roamed wild on a farm. The neighbours were half a mile away – unless you count coyotes and woodpeckers. They had happy adventures catching frogs and crickets, climbing snow drifts or getting caught out in the rain and hail.

The twins learned to entertain themselves reading a book on the evenings I had to finish a book review for the next morning. When there were power failures (and there *were* power failures every winter on the farm) we hardly worried about it. Reading stories aloud to the kids was more fun for them than television (it wasn't over in half an hour), and if I nodded off while reading, I'd keep talking anyways, sometimes causing weird changes to the plot and characters before being nudged awake. A short power failure meant the bedtime stories were told by candlelight, which was beautiful and creepy all at once. The power was never off for more than an hour or two, which is good considering the -40°C winters.

One bane of the home computer user is erratic power service. A surge protector can't do much when the power goes out, and when the lights brown out or flicker, it's time to shut off the computer and do electricity-free work.

I found this out the hard way, during a windstorm that blew down a few trees and made the power flicker. Half-way through an article on gardening, my old second-hand ADAM printer hesitated and began printing gibberish. Not just any gibberish, though – this looked like it almost made sense. Perhaps my word processor was translating my file into some arcane language known only to the ADAM Smartwriter program.

Bernie wandered over, coffee in hand, and inspected the printed article. "So," he commented, "Your ADAM processes words like our Braun food processor processes food."

It took a little poking around to figure out that the daisy wheel had gotten rotated and was now typing a few letters around the wheel from where it should, making yjr etpmh eptfd (if you know what I mean). It was like reading modern poetry by aphasics.

I couldn't find the right place to reset it manually, but turning the ADAM off and on put the daisy wheel back into the correct position. No more scrambled word salad and brown-out poetry now! And during storms I put my spiral-bound notebook to use instead, to write my own modern poetry.

Did our kids really need a computer of their own yet? They liked to type letters to Grandma and Grandpa on my machine. Ben got a pocket "video" game and took it apart to investigate. Lila learned to use the Public Library computers to find books by her favourite authors. I considered their current interests: that summer he was collecting pond life and she was illustrating her own stories.

The decision for that summer was to get our son a dip net ($2.99), our daughter some Plasticine ($3.99) and to let them type their stories and wildlife notes on my ADAM. I planned to get a new system ($many) with the money I earned from writing (dreams, I knew, but ya gotta dream). The ADAM would then be handed down to the kids, along with several game cartridges. For us, that looked like a better way to invest than a game machine.

The dream actually came through. It took a lot of book reviews and articles, but a year later I had enough saved for a Canon Starwriter. I even ponied up another $100 for a three year all-parts-and-services-included warranty. This machine would have to last until I sold a book.

The ADAM printer was almost completely worn out, by printing out three novels, two dozen short stories, plus articles and book reviews. But the computer itself still worked to play games and the "Learn to Type" program, and the kids still write letters on it. I found out later that my old typewriter, a big 1960 clunker I'd written three novels on and used all through University was still being used by a friend of a friend to make poetry books.

Now I have a new dream: to sell one or more of those five novels and buy a spiffy new machine that does everything but stamp the envelopes I'll send to the publishers. It can happen.

Dust to Dust

If, when I was a child, I ever said I was bored, my mother always had something for me to do. As a result, I'm never bored now. In just a few moments I can amazingly think of something to do. Usually I end up reading, writing e-mail to a friend, or taking a bath – none of the useful, productive things my mother used to recommend, like cleaning the bathroom or vacuuming, or writing stern but polite letters to government representatives.

It doesn't always work, though. The other night I had the house to myself. There were clean dishes for breakfast, cookies in the jar and I could still open and close the refrigerator/freezer doors without having to defrost a miniature glacier. To make things worse, that afternoon I had reviewed a book on public health care for a magazine, picked up my teenagers from the afterschool Drama Club and dropped their classmate at his home, and written to a relative. The last government representative I wrote to hadn't replied. All my regular duties were completed, and it was only eight pm.

I got bored.

I got so bored that I began dusting.

This may not seem like much to most people, who can coach sports teams and polish furniture every week. One of my friends swears his mother, a nurse, dusts even the tops of her door jambs – regularly. But then, she also irons her sheets and even sprays Lysol in her halls every morning. If I am ever seen ironing sheets or dusting the tops of door jambs, it means that I was kidnapped and re-programmed by aliens. I do clean house, of course. But I am also a charter member of Dusters Anonymous.

Dusters Anonymous is not a league of tall super-heroes in long black coats who combat high utility costs by fighting the privatization of public utilities. D.A. is a wonderful self-help group. When you feel the uncontrollable urge to dust the house, you telephone a friend. That way, you only end up dusting as far as the phone cord will reach. If she can't talk you out of it, you have to stop dusting when she gets there.

And she brings cheesecake.

So, at least the house gets partially dusted, and boredom is made better for a while. My latest Dusters Anonymous call, however, wasn't to some tall super-hero who could change my ceiling light bulbs to low-watt fluorescent bulbs, it was long distance to my friend Kris in another province. No cheesecake. No boredom, either, I have to admit, even if there were no super-heroes in long black coats saving the world. Kris tells great jokes, all world-weary, like:

Q: "How many Super-Moms does it take to dust off a light bulb?"

A: "Get real. Who dusts light bulbs?"

After that call, I finally had an excuse for not dusting the tops of my door jambs – I couldn't reach them with the phone tucked under my ear. The cord was too short to reach, and so was I.

And now I've also figured out the secret identity of one super-hero. She has risen from the ranks of homemakers and working women to speak out in defense of public schools, and public health care, and all the public sector that sustains a healthy economy of good citizens for our nation. She's got a sense of humour as inclusive as my friend Kris's light bulb jokes. She's Lois Hole, our Lieutenant-Governor, who gave a speech at Sturgeon Composite High School on Thursday night, at the twenty-fifth anniversary of the school she worked to build as a school board member.

This wasn't your run-of-the-mill praise for "Our School" but praise for public education, which brings together people from every background to learn skills and knowledge along with consideration and care for each other. This wasn't only the ordinary listing of a few people who worked hard to make visible results in one community, but a call to support not only public education but all the public sector. And Lois Hole wasn't just preaching to the choir. Her comments had added meaning, as the local MLA Dave Broda was seated in front of her.

Lois Hole, former Sturgeon school board member and chancellor of the University of Alberta, now looks a little frail, but she moves with vice-regal calm. She speaks with the confidence that comes from having no boss but the Queen and her conscience. "I thought the Lieutenant-Governor would be more... middle-of-the-road," murmured one teacher to me after Lois Hole's speech. This is middle-of-the-road, dear. The road's been moved out from under us, by education funding cutbacks and private clinics and privatized public utilities.

She doesn't wear a long black duster coat, but she's tall enough to change the light bulbs in my little house. And she's scrappy enough to tell the MLAs to clean house.

Costume

A lot of preparation goes on around here for Hallowe'en. Maybe that isn't the biggest festival on everybody's calendar, but it certainly is at our house. Monsters, scary things roaming around, scary places to explore as familiar places and things turn scary on a closer look. And then the release of laughter, as the monsters and scary things turn out to be jokes.

People need humour but they don't know what to do with it.

One of the high points on our family humour chart has to be my son's Hallowe'en costume when he was ten years old. He went as a barrel of toxic waste.

Weeks earlier he'd announced his goal. Luckily, I found a cardboard barrel at a dairy. My husband cut one end in a flap so our son's head could emerge from the supposed toxic barrel, and flaps on the sides so he could stick his hands out. With a flashlight inside, shining up through my daughter's blue scarf onto blue make-up and monster teeth, it was pretty impressive. But what made it work were the stickers that Uncle Karl made for it at work.

Oh yes, my brother worked in a sign shop. He was able to design and print up a large sticker reading "Toxic & Biohazardous Waste" complete with poison and biohazard symbols. In the correct colours, too – black on reflective yellow, though the letters were unofficially curly-cued.

It's amazing how scary and how recognizable warning symbols are: Fear This! Fear poison, fear disease, fear cancer, but then laugh at the image of what we fear on a silly costume. On the barrel, a couple more reflective biohazard stickers ensured night visibility. Fear the Dark! Fear monsters that come out of the Dark, but more practically, look out for children in the road.

And the crowning glory of the costume was the sticker that was a Material Safety Data Sheet. What kind of world is it where every substance in the workplace, even cedar or water, has a sheet of safety data? Well, it's a world where workers and managers can have easy access to safety information. And this sheet took itself less seriously. I reproduce it here:

"Material Safety Data Sheet

Guck, aka Bluck, aka $C_{23}H_{42}Pu_{239}O_2$

Warning: this drum contains biohazardous material, so for cry'n out loud don't touch it. I mean this is really vile stuff. The kind of hazardous waste that can turn the healthiest person into a shambling, rambling, gambling mutant who wears nothing but ripped gunny sacks & bangs on things with sticks for no readily apparent reason. If you happen to get some of this guck on you... well, I don't know what you should do. Maybe try putting a paper bag over your head or something. If you have to touch this waste, and I for one can't think of any good reason to do that, then wear about 15 pairs of rubber gloves, goggles, a respirator & one of those nifty tyvek suits they wear in the movies."

The effect was tremendous. Kids thought my son looked like a mutant. Adults looked at the stickers and shuddered. My daughter was delighted. She had to lead her brother around, make sure he didn't fall down the stairs when they were trick-or-treating, and took a cut of his candy. All in all, a complete success. We will have to go a long way to do any better.

That is, after we take our dead batteries and nearly-empty paint cans to the Toxic Round-up, empty our used motor oil into the oil recycling bin, get this year's immunization shots at the clinic and drop off the remnants of old prescription drugs at the pharmacy. We'll laugh once again at our stack of empty milk jugs strung onto a broom handle to make them easy to carry to the recycle bin, and at our armfuls of newspapers that when recycled, just might keep one more tree from being cut down.

People need humour, not only to help us face our fears, but to help us face the cleaning out of scary places, where monsters of our own making can result from the casual poisons used in our homes and work. We need to laugh at our luxuries, too, and take them less seriously than the responsibilities our luxuries bring. We can do a lot better, and then laugh for joy as well as relief.

In Season

The twins asked for Speculaas cookies this summer, but I explained that those are a seasonal cookie. We eat them only at Christmas time – St. Nicholas' Day, to be exact. The rush and expectations of Christmas get a little release on December 6 when Saint Nick makes a quick check around the house and bakes cookies with the dough we leave out for him.

Sure, the cookies are good, but Speculaas in August? It'd be like eating pumpkin pie in July when strawberries are ripe. I tried to tell the kids this, and I think they understood at least part of what I was saying. They asked for honey oatmeal cookies instead, which is why I ended up turning the kitchen into a jumbo-sized oven, baking cookies on a 92F day.

Funny how cookies which are baked too long kind of shrivel, while I stay the same size in all that heat… Must be all the taste testing. At any rate, it wasn't time to think about reducing. Not in August. Autumn is my time to take off a few pounds and get busy with my computer. All the strawberries are finished by then, so I've no excuse.

Some things are easier to do at the right time: lose weight, celebrate, go to school, do yard work, and homework. Sometimes the right thing is something that can be chosen, rather than imposed from outside. A lot of how we organize our children's home lives and schooling is based on a regular calendar of routines and events, lessons and holidays. We try to give choices within a frame of dependable routine: without a regular bedtime, the twins get wound up and exhausted, but without suppers out and evening visits, there would be no seeing our family and friends. We choose what our routine will be, as well as the changes we will make.

The twins had to adjust to visiting their great-grandparents in their apartment, rather than our house or Grandma's house, when the great-grandfather decided it was time to sell his car and stop driving. We had the easy adjustment – it was a pleasant walk to their apartment, especially for kids. He had the hard adjustment – calling cabs for trips to the Legion and buying groceries with a daughter playing chauffeur. It was a loss of independence for the great-grandparents, but they gave up maintaining a gas-guzzling car and spent about the same amount of money on cabs.

For him, it was time to stop driving; and it didn't take a major accident to convince him. (Only a wee fender bender in a parking lot, honest.) For the rest of the family, we have to make time, once in a while, to be their chauffeurs. The children try to keep their backseat games quieter when it's our turn to drive. That's our part; and I think it helps our kids to see how family doesn't focus only on the children's needs, but on each of us in our own time. The twins are old enough to be quiet when Great-Grandpa has his hearing aid on, and even big enough to pass platters around the table at dinner.

We had a big family lunch on the farm during the summer, with kids, uncle and aunt and a great-uncle around the table with both leaves in for the occasion. After eating, the kids ran off to play with the aunt's dog; my husband Bernie and I drove out to the back field with his brother and uncle. The trunk was opened to reveal locked firearm cases and boxes of ammunition.

"Got the clay targets?" asked the uncle, holding out a spring-handle for throwing clay disks. He brought out a .22 rifle and a light shotgun and the four of us began target practise. Neither of the young men made fun of my beginner's clumsiness – compared with their uncle, we all had a lot to learn. He never missed, except when I threw the target so that it rolled into the field of peas instead of flying into the cloudless sky. Once in a while the wind carried the twins' voices all the way out from the house.

The rifle and shotgun were as fine as rosewood and metal sculptures. "These are my best," the uncle said while reloading. "I'll be taking most of my collection to my son in Ontario this fall. Since my by-pass surgery, I've felt better, but it's time to hand them on."

My accuracy improved a little, with practise and instruction from the uncle. He put his arms around mine, showing me how to hold the shotgun, and I noticed that his hairline was thinning but the same as Bernie's hairline; and his hands were wrinkled but as long and straight as Bernie's brother's hands. Together we aimed the shotgun over the field of ripening peas, dusty in the late summer sun. Far behind us the twins were playing; one with that same hairline, the other with long, straight hands. Their voices came faintly through a thicket of aspens that were just beginning to turn golden with the first hint of the seasons turning to autumn.

It was the uncle's turn for a last round of target shooting. He looked at his nephews with the box of targets and the handle. "Pull!" The clay disk arced up into the wind and blue sky, and was shattered.

Taking An Interest In Money

Money is an interesting concept for children. When they were small, my kids picked up pennies from gutters, squirreled coins into piggy banks and studied the pictures on the backs of dollar bills in varying denominations. "This one's got a kingfisher, and this one has some men on horses all standing in a circle!"

"If you're finished looking, I want my money back. All of it!" Sometimes I had to watch them like a hawk, because even when little, both kids became as interested in money as a Minister of Finance.

They counted nickels and pennies and ran their hands through piles of coins like Midas must have done as a child. Elaborate plans were made, to save money and buy... anything! Anything they might want. They even tried imitating the cartoon Donald Duck's rich Uncle Scrooge, but they didn't have enough money to burrow into – and they decided that throwing money into the air and letting it hit them on the head must be easier on cartoon heads than in real life.

Sore heads never put them off planning, saving or scheming new ways to earn money. Even at seven years old, they were already becoming successful entrepeneurs. That summer my daughter Lila potted bedding plants into hanging baskets with her Oma and sold them at the farmers' markets. My son Ben helped make, package and sell brightly coloured play-dough. The markets had two small vendors, who learned the prices at our vegetable table and how to make change, before they lost their baby teeth.

The kids are grown now, and know what to do with money once they actually have some. My daughter has a sensible part-time job making sandwiches. It pays all her bills, and leaves her enough studying time to stay on the honour roll at school. My son makes punk and goth fashion accessories to sell when he's at school, or in town, or (sigh!) on the Greyhound bus to visit the grandparents. When someone says "Hey, cool studded armbands!" he has found a customer for the dog collars and badges in his bag.

But does an entrepreneur who sells armbands and dog collars understand the merits of higher education? Lila has always planned to go to University, but Ben hasn't settled on a plan. To give him a little more motivation as well as a day's work, I took him to help my sister-in-law on sheep-shearing day at her farm.

The shearer watched my son help drive sheep into the barn, into smaller stalls, and then grab each one to be sheared. "Why did you bring your son to help this year?" he asked.

"We want him to go to University," I explained.

"Ah." We watched Ben, smeared with wool grease and flecks of straw, struggle with a ram that weighed more than he did. "Show him the alternative. Good plan."

It's not that hard to teach growing kids to save money for University tuition as well as spend money on treats. If only it were as easy for us all to have that much fiscal responsibility on the scale of provincial and federal governments! Perhaps deficit financing can sometimes make as much sense as a mortgage for a family home. But it had better be planned carefully enough to make a family's financial plans look like the plots of a seven-year-old with a handful of nickels. I guess that University is pretty far ahead when you're only seven, and money in the pocket jingles so attractively right now.

I remember a day when my seven-year-old walked across his Oma's kitchen, jingling, with his hands cupped together. "Have you got money?" I asked. "Put it in a pocket or you'll lose it."

"I don't have a pocket, Mom," he said, jingling as he walked.

"I'll put it in my pocket for you," I said, and held out my hands.

He put what he was holding into my hands. "My money's in my sock," he said cheerfully, and sat down on the floor to pull off the grubby sock. "I just gave you a toad."

My son now knows more about responsibility, as well as saving. My daughter is making budgets and shopping lists. I don't think I'll worry too much about them yet; I will have to be prepared in the future, though. I assume that the first time my kids buy a car will be a lot harder for me to handle than the toad ever was.

If This is New Year's, We Must Be at Grandma's House

We overdid the planning one year. Back in Victoria for a few weeks at the Christmas season, we tried to see everybody and do everything we'd been missing out on. It got so we even planned what shoes to wear to Aunty Kris' place so we all could go to the park later.

This is something Bernie warns me about – I have a tendency to organize the entire family beyond efficiency. Nazi Mom tends to take over everyone's free time. But we really did want to get a lot of things done, and if we just thought about it a little, we could do everything! Especially if we did it my way. I was used to being the one who organized the kids when Bernie was away in Victoria for his furniture course. We began organizing things together, and it worked. Boy, were we organized!

There were the standard visits to three married couples with children (not only because they're our friends, but all our kids get along for an afternoon playing in a pack). We buzzed through Chinatown getting a few more presents and a bag of fortune cookies, and picked up some cheese-oregano buns at the Rising Star Bakery. We climbed on the concrete creations at Cadboro Bay and took a cousin's kid with us to Goldstream Park and Little Niagara Falls, all wreathed in ice on Boxing Day. We visited a friend who had had cancer and was now in remission, and went to family parties. We did it all.

On New Year's Day we went to Mount Douglas Beach to take a break from all the people. The seven-year-old twins were relieved to run and holler after being so quiet at their grandparents' house. I didn't realize how thoroughly our holiday had become organized in great detail until my daughter Lila ran ahead and crowed: "That's exactly what I've been looking for ever since we came here!" She picked up a long sea whip of kelp.

"What are you going to do with that?" I asked her.

"Drag it around after us while we walk down the beach," Lila said, matter-of-fact. She thought for a moment. "Then, *hurl* it into the air. And if it doesn't go completely back into the water, I'll *stomp* it to death." And as we walked along the beach, finding stones and raccoon footprints, she did just as she planned, carefully and with great satisfaction.

(We hung around the beach for a while. Dinner was late that evening. Nobody minded.)

Inside the magic wand

Have you seen those magic wands? You know, the ones that look like clear glass with a swirl of star and moon-shaped sequins, and colourful glitter that flows from end to end in a clear liquid. The wands come in a couple of sizes, down to key-chain size. They have a lot of appeal for little kids and doting aunties (and mothers waiting for the laundry to finish drying). If you've got one of these toys, you've probably played with it for longer than you'd care to admit.

Did you ever wonder what was inside them? But no, you'd never break one. The wands aren't exactly cheap, after all, and who could break a kid's toy, or help a budding scientist risk eye injury on the sharp pieces? Nope, I had to hide my own curiosity and just play with the sparkly thing when I could get it away from my kids.

But for... er, purely scientific reasons, I can report the results of an accident... nope, let's call it an experiment that happened one winter at our home.

1. The wand is thick, heavy plastic that breaks with very sharp edges if left out in -40°C temperatures. (Oops.)

2. The liquid is mineral oil.

3. The "glitter" is small plastic balls of incredibly bright colours. The sequins are, yep, sequins.

4. The oily sparkly bits cling to *everything*.

Hats

Do people wear hats much any more? Well, maybe ball caps in summer. But real hats like a fedora or a pillbox hat? No, only that Canadian icon, the toque is still worn. And mostly by Canadians. My brother once had to tell American friends what a toque is. "It's a knitted hat that looks really doofusy until you've been outside without one for more than six seconds."

I haven't worn a toque this winter. Every day I wear my Grandpa's wool cap with the collar turned down over my ears. It is really warm and doesn't muss my hair as much as a toque. I like the brim which keeps snowflakes out of my eyes. This is the best hat for cold weather.

I traded hats with Grandpa, not to get his, but to give him the other. Grandpa's eighty-seven, living in Victoria, where winter is mild. He walks a lot, but he doesn't look around for cars. "I've been crossing this street for years," he says. "People ought to know by now." So I gave him my husband's Day-Glo orange ball cap. It's visible a block away in the rain. I'd rather give him a yellow firefighter's helmet with a flashing red light. But he likes a good hat he can stuff in a pocket.

It's nice to have his good hat since I lost my velvet Chinese hat in Toronto on my shoestring book tour in May. That pretty little hat was warm enough for mild days but not for forty below. I got a new Chinese hat in Chinatown.

Not that I needed a new hat. This Christmas my brother and his wife sent us new ball caps from where he works. These have the name of a computer game embroidered in red and black: *Ripley's Believe It Or Not*. There was also the game, which we will enjoy when my husband Bernie soups up our computer. He wears the Computer Fix-it hat around our house.

My spouse Bernie also wears toques and coveralls and a layer of gasoline, working outdoors for an environmental business. He recovers spilled gasoline from under old gas stations, pumping it up through pipes. He notices on cold days he feels particularly cold. His clothing freezes stiff with gasoline evaporating colder than ice. Even his toque is a gas-sicle. When he comes home he can't dry his gear by the furnace. He'll set his hat on fire.

It was so cold this morning I bundled the kids up like bear cubs in hoods and all. Well, I tried to. They had colds and went back to bed. They just didn't want to catch the schoolbus at 7:45 on a -30 morning. But after a while my son realized that he had just finished his library book. My daughter wanted to act out a shampoo ad with friends in Language Arts. Staying home wasn't going to be much fun. Their colds got better all of a sudden. On with the snow gear and I tied their hoods snug. Bernie played chauffeur and drove them to school. He didn't put on a chauffeur's hat though. I checked.

Then on with my writer's hat and into my office on our farm near Legal. Actually it's nearer a hamlet called Fedorah, which seems appropriate. I should write a mystery story with men in fedora hats.

Having Our Cake

We each have things we're better at, Bernie and I, but we make it a point of pride that each of us is not only *able* to do most of the necessary work to maintain our household, but we both actually *do* this work where the kids can benefit from our good example. None of this "men do outdoors maintenance, women keep house" cliché for us.

Of course, this does result in days when my daughter Lila and I are leaning into a car engine, checking the dipstick and asking Bernie where the motor oil is kept. It also results in conversations like one we had this morning.

Bernie called me away from my desk. "Oh darling, light of my life, woman of my dreams – may I consult your expertise on a matter of which you have greater experience?"

Flattery *and* compliments! I left the word processor humming to itself and went to look up the stairs at Bernie and our daughter, home from school with a cold.

"This cake mix says 'Rich recipe uses 3 eggs and 1 cup of oil. Can I use olive oil?" he asked.

"Sure, it'll work, but there's canola oil in the cans cupboard," I suggested. "Olive oil might taste different."

"It's a chocolate cake, who'll notice?"

"Taste it. If you notice, don't use it."

I was already turning back to my desk when Bernie called again. "I've got some 10W30 we could try!"

"Oh yeah, taste that!" Back to work with a chuckle.

Our daughter came down in a few minutes, dusted with flour. "I washed my hands real good and Daddy let me help with his cake. Daddy knows everything about making cakes. He even knows how to make one round and one square cake!"

This is the real benefit of sharing the work around the house. Sure, it was my turn last time to put a litre of oil into the car. But now I get to go eat a cake I didn't have to bake, frost or clean up after.

Four Ways

Four Ways to Make Your Phone Ring:
1. Get half-way through changing a baby and reach for the diaper creme.
2. While carving a jack o'lantern, begin scooping the goop out of the pumpkin.
3. When a family member asks you a sensitive question about your feelings, think carefully about your answer.
4. Apply shampoo to your wet hair and begin lathering.

FOUR WAYS TO KEEP YOUR Phone From Ringing:
1. Buy an answering machine.
2. Record an outgoing message more sensible than: "Hi, I'm not home, so come over and steal my answering machine and other appliances."
3. Get a second phone line for your computer or answering machine, or teenager - whichever gets more calls than you do.
4. Resolve to make conversation with the next human being who tries to make contact.

FOUR WAYS TO MAKE SURE your car starts easily this morning:
1. Have no appointments for today or tomorrow.
2. Bring along someone who knows more about cars than you do.
3. Wear clothing suited for leaning into a greasy engine or crawling under it.
4. Read a book on Car Maintenance Tips.

FOUR WAYS TO MAKE SURE your car won't start in the morning:

1. Wait till the last possible minute before leaving the house.
2. Load up everything you're planning to take and get all your passengers to buckle up before you turn the key.
3. Develop an alarming case of cabin fever and decide to drive to downtown because you've run out of manicure scissors.
4. Take a phone call from someone special who is waiting at the airport for a ride.

FOUR WAYS TO HAVE A perfect family dinner:

1. Call your spouse's mother and get her recipe for your spouse's favourite home-cooked dish.
2. Borrow a library book on new ways to prepare your family's favourite vegetable.
3. Find all the napkins that match your good tablecloth, then iron and fold them into swans.
4. Ten minutes before dinner is served, lock any pets up and check that everybody's clothes and hands are clean - that includes yourself.

FOUR WAYS TO HAVE A perfectly fine family dinner:

1. Thaw out a vegetarian casserole that you made a double batch of last week and froze half when everybody ate all of the other half.
2. Cover it with grated cheese and bacon and heat it in the oven with a frozen pizza.
3. Put out mugs and shot glasses, a jug of milk and a jug of V-8, and insist that everybody tries your new way to make boilermakers.
4. Serve apples and Mr. Freezes for dessert.

FOUR WAYS TO HAVE A summer yard party:

1. Put all the small children in the back yard and give them each two chocolate-covered espresso beans.

WORKING PARENT

2. Put all the adults on the back porch to watch the show.
3. Try to finish cooking dinner while everybody else is entertained.
4. Give everybody tall drinks of ice water in hopes that they won't get thirsty and request complicated drinks or hungry and notice how long it took to get some kind of dinner on the table.

FOUR WAYS TO AVOID ever having a yard party:
1. Put a sign reading "Mine Field" at the edge of your lawn.
2. If the police come round to ask questions, admit that it's more of an un-mowed lawn than a field, but it is indeed yours.
3. Replace the sign with another that says "Mosquito Sanctuary."
4. Tell your relatives that you're thinking of throwing a barbecue again - the last time it went only twenty-two feet.

FOUR WAYS TO FIND A great book:
1. Go to your smartest friend's house and ask to use the bathroom, where you'll find a book.
2. Go to the library and look through the books on the re-shelving trolley.
3. Stand up on a bus, transit train or airplane and ask everybody to hold up whatever they're reading.
4. If someone's water pipes break and soak a bookshelf, the wettest book will be the best and most interesting one.

FOUR WAYS TO FIND SOMETHING to read when you need it desperately:
1. Look in the glove compartment for your car owner's manual.
2. Practise pronouncing all the ingredients listed on your food labels.
3. If far-sighted, take off your glasses and stand behind somebody reading the newspaper, to read over his or her shoulder.
4. If near-sighted, put on your glasses and spill your bag at the feet of somebody reading a newspaper.

My Goal as a Writer

The year ahead is shaping up to be a pretty good year. Oh sure, the weather is too cold for comfort. But my work as a freelance writer is going well. I have to set my own goals and meet them as well as I can. Some of what I write even sells to publishers.

I've got a new book coming out in the coming fall. I'll take notes for another book when my family goes fossil hunting in summer. But I just met one of my personal goals as a writer. I cracked up CBC radio host Vicki Gabereau on the air.

Oh sure. It's not like no one else can do it. But it was a goal I had as a writer. For years I listened to the *Gabereau* show. Mostly I listened while typing stories during the twins' naptime. Some day one of those authors getting interviewed would be me! If I could write a book for a publisher, I could get interviewed on her show. And I could make her laugh that full-voiced laugh.

But when my first book came out, Vicki was all "booked out" for the season. Her producer, Doug Tuck, was really nice when he said I wouldn't get interviewed.

Then he called me the other day. No, it wasn't to set up an interview at the last minute. "You sent in a letter when we asked listeners for recipes," Doug Tuck said. "We read and recorded it for broadcast tomorrow. I think you'll want to listen," he suggested, as cool as a secret agent in a conspiracy.

You can bet I tuned in to the *Gabereau* show the next day. Doug and Vicki's voices came out of my kitchen table radio, reading recipes. They came to my letter, and the recipe I got from my aunty.

Now, my aunty is some kinda woman. Vicki ploughed through my description of aunty as cheerfully as she could. I'm a long-winded writer. And it was the first time Vicki had seen my letter, with aunty's recipe for Popcorn Stuffing for turkey.

"Pour in the popcorn and pin the openings shut tightly with turkey skewers," Vicki read aloud gamely. "Bake it in the oven at 375 degrees F until the popcorn blows the ass off the turkey ... and fills up the kitchen!"

She broke up completely. From giggles all the way to a belly laugh. Then she howled at her producer. "And that's why you wanted *me* to read it. You tricked me!"

It is a small victory for a writer. It has nothing like the prestige of a Governor-General's award, or the Booker Prize or the Nobel. But at least my joke got shared across the country on national radio. And I cracked up someone whose humour I've enjoyed for years.

Now I'm writing to the *Gabereau* show's producer about my new book. They may not interview me for this book either. But at least I can tell them the one about the writer and the turkey who walked into an espresso bar...

Celebrating Christmas

We go through a lot getting ready for Christmas. All the preparations, the gifts, the visiting, the reverent hours in church or on long walks outdoors, all of it adds up to one heck of a lot of getting ready and very little actual celebrating.

There was a little celebrating going on at the school concert, though. First of all, we were all celebrating actually arriving at the school during a blizzard that blew snowdrifts across the road while we watched and skidded. I did phone the school before we left home, to see if the concert was cancelled on account of weather. "Oooh, we really ought to," said the nice young man at the school office. "Have you seen the snow blowing out there? But there's no way we can phone everybody, so we'll just go ahead with however many make it." Almost everybody turned up, and by the time we got there the building was full of people, wet winter clothes, and 800 snowboots by the doors.

It used to be that you could tell teachers from parents because the teachers wore three-piece suits. Even the women. Now teachers seem to wear what everybody else wears. (I wonder what that says about the economy?) But I could tell us apart in the crowd. The teachers wore shoes, while parents padded around in socks, damp from the snowy footprints inside the door.

I like Christmas concerts. I like the pageants, and the secular carols, and the concert band playing something classical. I got us seats up front, where Bernie began to doze inside his big warm car coat. "Nudge me when it begins," he whispered.

He woke up when the first carol rang out, applauded Ben as a five-foot high gingerbread man, and praised Lila singing in the choir. He pointed out to me that the stage crew looked like real roadies, in their rock star tour t-shirts. Generally, I'd have to say Bernie had a good time.

A particularly good time, during the singing of The Huron Carol, where the "hunter braves" with their plaid flannel shirts and fibreglass bows drew nigh to a cradle draped in skins of purple, yellow and lime-green fun fur. So that's why Lila borrowed my craft supplies!

But Bernie had entirely too much fun during the acting out of "Grandma Got Run Over By a Reindeer." This time he couldn't hold in the giggles till the lights went down. Threatening to stifle his red-faced laughter with my scarf had no effect. Luckily, there weren't many disapproving stares, and none at all from the vice-principal, who was busy a minute later leading an energetic combo in the theme from Peter Gunn.

Now that's some kinda vice-principal, who can play electric guitar with the students! I like the kind of concert where all the kids participate, and emerging talents shine amid all the fun. It's great when the parents enjoy the celebration too, even as much as Bernie did, sitting up front where everyone could see and hear him enjoy a perfect view of the pageant's Grandma as she got run over by that reindeer.

Next year he has to sit at the back of the auditorium.

I am Curious... George

We're watching television again. (Oh, horrors! Isn't hiking and fishing enough?) No, but we're not watching network television, at least. TV commercials are enough to turn our brains into porridge and lead to our children making observations like: "This ad says if you buy this car, the pretty lady will ride with you and be your friend." You know, there's not much you can say about that except "Yup" or "I dunno about that. We drive an old beater. Can you say *beater*? I think you can," in true Mr. Rogers' style.

But television has other purposes besides teaching us what material goods to covet. It keeps kids quiet.

Too much TV time uses up all our kids' ability to sit still and makes them hyper for the rest of the day. But if we let them watch a Faerie Tale Theatre video at the end of a busy day, they sleep like angels. So it's understandable that lately we've been haunting the video rack at the local public library, and borrowing videos from my brother and sister-in-law's collection.

The videos we've been borrowing are definitely of two natures. There are the animated shows for the kids, and old science fiction monster movies for the whole family. (We just love to get together and watch Godzilla tear apart Tokyo.) Then there are the other movies for me and Bernie.

They don't come with lurid covers and titles like "Sorority Vampires" or "Hot Victims". No, that stuff doesn't have much appeal after reading the paper and hearing "The World at Six" on CBC Radio. We aren't borrowing racey skin movies, either; it's awfully hard to explain to the kids that the three movies we're borrowing from Uncle Karl and Auntie Stephanie are *Care Bears, Godzilla meets Rhodan*, and *Something For Mom And Dad With A Title I Can't Read To You*.

So you know what we end up watching by ourselves?

Chinese Cooking. How to Start a Home Business. Router Bits and Jigs for Fine Woodworking.

Today we watched *West Coast Trail: a Hiker's Guide* while reading the *Globe and Mail*, then rushed to return the video to the library before it closed. Does entertainment get much better? I hope so.

Sometimes I'm tired of watching *Curious George* and think wistful thoughts about *I am Curious... Yellow*. What are the movies doing with Adult Entertainment and Mature Themes these days, I wonder? But then yesterday after I walked my brother's dogs, I popped *Sex Trek: The Next Penetration* into his VCR. Sure, it was funny seeing an actor with Vulcan ears playing Mr Spock in a skin movie. But I left the silly thing in the VCR, he found it when he came home, and now I'll never hear the end of it. It may have been an adult video, but it sure wasn't a "mature" theme. But come to think of it, how did it end up in *his* collection?

I think I'll stick to Godzilla videos. At least when the kids come home, tell me about their day at school and ask "What did *you* do today?" I can honestly say, "I borrowed a movie we can share." Already I'm craving some Kool-aid and hot buttered popcorn.

Feedback

The give and take of mutual feedback keeps us together, friends and family. Knowing how we look in each others' eyes makes us keep trying to be better. We learn by teaching the children and hearing back from them the lessons we drummed into their heads as well as the things we inadvertently taught them along the way...

I hadn't realized how they pick things up until Ben wanted a desk for his room one day – and made one out of a few pieces of scrap lumber and ten-penny nails. He knew where Daddy kept the tools and wood. I also didn't realize that one of the side effects of taking turns making up endless verses for old folk songs would be that both kids can compose poetry and recite famous poems by heart. (Ahah! All those poetry readings I dragged the kids to are paying off!)

The really great part about this is that the twins think it is normal to be able to design furniture, drive a tractor, make up poems, cook lunch, use a computer, and babysit. After all, everybody they know can do all these things, and so could the twins at nine years old. (Is that what I've been teaching the kids? Holy cow, talk about positive feedback! Some of this parent stuff is working out just fine.)

Some feedback comes at a slower pace, at the speed of my first book's glacial progress towards a publisher and the printed page. Bernie had read the manuscript already, but he still had comments to make when I proofread the galleys.

"I'm not so sure I like the way you characterized me in this one piece." Bernie looked uncertain.

"What didn't you like?"

"You said I had 'the intensity of a television preacher and the charm of a carny barker,'" he complained.

Oh yeah. I remembered that one. I also called him a one-man committee, as I recalled. "Well," I suggested, "would you rather I said that you had the charm of a television preacher and the intensity of a carny barker?"

"Good Lord, no!" He shuddered. "I guess I can't complain too much." He knew why, too... he'd see his complaints the next time I needed inspiration for a new chapter. Everything can end up being new material.

My mother's reaction to reading about events she saw from her own point of view is complex, and not easy to summarize. Maybe she was struck by what parts of what events I choose to write about. Or maybe it's what I feel easy talking about that would never occur to her to reveal.

Nevertheless, she did have a comment to make on Bernie's Last Word for my first book (his afterword was called: "Yes I Shaved My Kid's Head). Mom lit up a cigarette when she put down the galleys. "He didn't write about the mother-in-law's viewpoint on his son's haircut," she said, tapping the galleys with one long, elegant fingernail.

"What was that, Mom?" I asked, expecting an opinion on whether we ought to have let our son walk around looking like an egg with a weasel pelt draped over it.

"Well, I came home and found you sitting in the kitchen with your head in your hands," she said. (At the time, we were living in Mom and Dad's house on the Island.) "I asked how you were, and you said, 'Fine. I'm just having a migraine.' Then I heard the electric hair razor buzzing downstairs."

Her grin was infectious; I started to laugh.

"I went downstairs, and saw the haircut," she went on. "I thought, no WONDER she's having a migraine, her husband is shaving her son's head." Mom flicked away a cigarette ash, and with it any sense of criticism, but not the humour. "Did you make enough scalloped potatoes for all of us?" she asked. "I put a pot roast in. Let's all have dinner together tonight."

Home is where, according to Robert Frost, when you have to go there, they have to let you in. Home for me is where, when you talk about people in your stories they still talk TO you after reading what you wrote.

Too Normal for Radio

Life will never be the same since my first book, *No Parent is an Island*, reached the bookstores. Long years of being an unknown writer are now over – if the book succeeds, whatever "successful" really is. By the end of the first week in print, one radio station had already said they wouldn't interview me because the book isn't interesting enough to enough people. But CBC Radio's *Basic Black* wouldn't interview me because the book is too... normal.

This was a surprise. Never in my life has anyone accused me of being too normal. Oh, perhaps a little *bourgeois* for some of my friends in University, or kind of whitebread compared to my fellow low-income writers. But my farming neighbours in Alberta never call me normal. At a barbecue last summer, one neighbour got up the courage to ask me, "Are you one of them *artist* types?"

"Well, I'm a writer," I answered.

"I knew it! I knew you was one of them artist types," he said. "You wear different clothes, you talk so different, you don't cut your hair or drink beer. You always work in the garden and mail letters in town instead of farming or working in the city. My wife thought you must be a hippie, but I said, 'Don't jump to conclusions. Maybe *she's* just one of them artist types.'"

Now I'm too normal for *Basic Black*. I dunno. If a book that ends with my pagan husband shaving our son's head is too normal, maybe I'd have better luck with a science fiction novel. After all, that same month one of my stories was up for the Aurora, the Canadian science fiction award. The winner was announced on Mother's Day at the national SF convention, after I presented an academic paper on "The role of the parent-child relationship among characters in Canadian science fiction."

"Too normal for public radio?" my father snorted when he heard the news. "You've never been normal. You oughta wear your little Chinese hat when you go on your book tour."

"This is Paula for sure," said my sister-in-law. "Too different for the normal people and too normal for the different people. She just has to keep making her own group like always."

Perhaps faulty promotion is to blame. Maybe the biographical notes should mention that I run naked on the farm, where I am semi-vegetarian but prefer to kill my own chickens rather than buy meat from the grocery; or that most of my writing for three years was typed one-handed while cuddling one or the other of my twins. That's interesting, even to normal people... isn't it?

And if it isn't, well, tough luck. Long ago I gave up trying to live up or down to someone else's average score. And in the drive to be unusual, it's hard to compete with people who use ultralight airplanes to teach geese how to migrate. I'm going to keep writing science fiction and nonfiction, and I've got complete confidence that as always, I can't make up stories as strange as what really happens in the world around me.

At the Legion

When my parents joined their local branch of the Legion in Victoria, BC, I was worried. Why would they need to join a club that just sits around in a pub? That was it, as far as I could see: they were officially old. One foot in the grave. And they would put the other foot in there too, by smoking and drinking all day at the Legion. I thought my parents had forgotten everything they taught me about community recreation, and sports teams and having fun.

Then one rainy night I ventured into the Legion for the first time, to pick up my folks when they'd had a pint. And I discovered that my worries were not well founded. Half of the old guys were women. And one of them set me up with a pint of ginger ale. Of course, designated drivers get coffee or soft drinks at any pub. But they also brought my Dad a fruit juice. You see, he'd had a heart attack a while ago. Some people on the Legion's curling teams drink fruit juice because they're on heart medication, so the bar carries juice. They didn't forget.

My Mom and Dad were celebrating balancing the branch's books in time to start planning the Christmas dinner. "We had to account for all the money we raised," my Mom said. "And the local charities we gave it to, and what they did with it. Look, here are the thank-you letters telling us how their projects went! Our branch members buying 50-50 tickets and all, we raised over $25,000 for charities." Mom didn't forget the account book and letters when we headed home. Dad didn't forget the Christmas planning folder.

Dad got me to type out some Christmas carols for the folder. There's a lot of plans in that folder. Christmas dinner at the Legion isn't for members, like I expected. It's for the Veterans who live in the hospital. Some of those soldiers never did come home from war, for the rest of their lives. For some of the men, this is their only outing of the year. So Christmas at the Legion for them happens every year, for sure, with turkey dinner with gravy and all the trimmings. There are slippers and so on for presents, and songs carolled by women in red sweaters. They never forget the old songs.

So when my parents asked me to help with the Poppy Drive, we all spent our mornings at the new Legion, down where Victoria's Inner Harbour meets the Gorge. Dozens of volunteers were busy pinning thousands of poppies to cards and stuffing them into envelopes, counting and bundling them to be mailed out, seeking donations for the veterans still in hospital, and their widows and orphans.

There wasn't a beer in sight, just coffee, and smokers kept to one room of the air-conditioned building. Cheerful talk filled the bright rooms, as my Dad consulted and chattered with the men. The women at my table kept up a lively stream of pleasant talk, my Mom's hands moving as busy as a knitter. A latecomer put away his bus pass and asked if we had room for him at our table. But we insisted: everyone sitting at our table has to tell a funny story. Instantly, he forgot all his funny stories. So we told one about him, while he began pinning poppies. And we laughed together. Lest we forget.

Top This

I find the oddest things when cleaning up. Not that cleaning happens often enough, but the oddest things sure do turn up.

Tonight our living room (in the downstairs of my parents' house) looks like a bomb went off in it. All right, it often looks that way, but this time is particularly bad. Three times this week I've cleaned the "Writing: Current" pile off the deep freeze next to my typing table, but it's bigger than ever tonight. Bernie just sorted his tools to make room for the desk he glued and clamped this afternoon, but there wouldn't be room to walk between the door and the couch if the kids hadn't put away their bike helmets and knapsack... without being asked. Something must be going on, if the kids are putting stuff away without being asked.

Something *is* going on. I found a grocery bag full of hair in the bathroom when I came home this afternoon.

Actually, that wasn't the first thing I saw after a hard day flogging my first book at various bookstores around town. "Hi, honey, I'm home," I called as I stepped around tools and wood.

A voice out of the woodworking shop answered mildly: "Brace yourself."

"That's what Stephanie said at her gas station when I pulled in to fill the tank." I put away keys, briefcase and coat. "I asked her what for, and all she would tell me was 'No, it's nothing to do with hospitals.' So what am I bracing for?" Coming into the woodworking shop, the reason caught me flatfooted.

Bernie had shaved his head.

My Woodstock Generation partner with the ponytail was bald as an egg.

Sure, he'd talked about cutting his hair – even about shaving his head "for a change." This was sure a change! Bernie hadn't cut his hair for twelve years, not since the brush cut when he was in the Reserves. For a moment I couldn't decide if he looked more like his Uncle Henry or Mr. Clean.

"I'm gonna get you a bigger earring," was one of the first things I said. "So you can look like a pirate." Another of the first things was: "That looks really good – you've got the ears for it." Remember those two responses, humour and a compliment, because Bernie is fixating on the other thing I said. "Have you talked with the doctor since you went off your medication?"

It was a fair question! Years earlier, one of Bernie's friends had shaved his own head—sat down on the centre line between six lanes of traffic and shaved half his head and half his beard with a straight razor. Then he burnt the pile of hair. Then he checked himself into the local Institute for a week or so.

Bernie pointed out that this wasn't that kind of head-shaving. He hadn't burnt the pile of hair, for one thing, and for another, he'd used our Deluxe Home Barber Set. It wasn't something to get bent out of shape about. He let me touch the springy bristles, and the kids did too, when they came home.

Ben's reaction was forty seconds of wide-eyed silence while his father said hi and asked him how was his day. Eventually he demanded: "Who are you and what have you done with my dad?" (He'll be a professional comedian one day, for sure.) Lila, however, opted for the classic question, "Huhh – why did you shave your head?"

Bernie handed her some line about chemotherapy making it all fall out, but she wasn't having any of that. Instead she made comments about his hairline, and asked how he got the scar on top of his head. "Falling down the stairs at Knitting Grandma's house when I was seven," she was told. The kids seemed disappointed that it wasn't from some sort of *tough* experience.

I withdrew from the scene to the kitchen to mix lemonade. Later Bernie found me upstairs relaxing with a cold lemonade and plenty of ice, drinking out of a fishbowl.

"Couldn't find a big enough glass," I said when he did a double take.

"You did this on purpose," he stammered.

"I was thinking the other day about the farm, and the hammock on hot days, and got the fishbowl clean and ready to take to the farm with us this summer. Did you know there's a restaurant down on Wharf Street that serves frozen margaritas in these?"

"You've been planning this," he accused me with delight. "You got it ready and hid it so you could weird me out."

"Hey." I sipped from the chilled fishbowl. "Sometimes planning's not enough."

Bernie got lots of other reactions, too. Our son's friend came over to meet Ben for skateboarding and froze at the sight of the bald apparition at the door. My mother didn't recognise him at first. There was quite a flap when she looked out the window and saw him in the back yard. And yes, there were reactions from passers-by. When Bernie walked down to the bank machine at the supermarket, a couple of kids came by and yelled, "Hey, Baldy – get outa here!"

Never missing a beat, Bernie leaned out the bank's door and yelled back: "I'm not bald – I get my hair cut this way, you little punks!"

One of the kids looked back. "It wasn't me, I didn't say it!"

"I know," Bernie told him. "It was your friend. So I figure you'll tell him."

"Oh." The kid shrugged. "Okay." In an era of urban violence and drive-by shootings, it's nice to know there's still a place where a man with a shaved head and a kid in baggy jeans can understand each other. It would be even nicer if I could understand Bernie even a little more often. I can't always have a fishbowl stashed in the cupboard for when it's needed.

Beg Pardon?

It was a cold winter's day. My family was trapped indoors by temperatures below -30C. I made a cup of tea and was hunched over it, trying to get warm. Then Ben came up behind me.

"Mom," he said. He waited for me to look up. I didn't really want to. That teacup was the warmest thing in the house. I wanted to marry it, but knew that the attraction wouldn't last.

My son was still waiting patiently when I eventually looked up at him. "Mom," he said again, in case I wasn't really paying attention yet. Then he asked, "Do you ever find that reality distracts you?"

Huh? It was a long time before my brain and mouth got co-ordinated enough to ask him, "From *what*?"

"You know," he said. "From what you're really doing."

What could he be really doing that reality could distract him from? "Like what?" I said after a while.

"Oh, you know," he said, standing on one foot. "Like when you want to use the computer but it's not working. Or when you're watching TV but Dad says it's time to go. Or when you get your skateboard fixed but there's too much snow to go skateboarding."

"You mean when *you* want to go skateboarding," I said, and drank from my teacup. "One can use the impersonal verb form when one is speaking to one's mother. And you can too. But you don't have to be so formal when you talk to your friends."

"You know what I mean," said Ben. "The real stuff that you're thinking about, that you do but sometimes you can't. Like, I can't climb trees now because it's too cold."

The teacup was getting cold in my hand. While I glared into my cup, my sneaky kid stole a handful of chocolate chips from the jar in the cupboard. Then he went off to read Michael Crichton novels and play with his toy dinosaurs. I drank the rest of my tea and thought about what he had said.

I now had an amazing insight into his thoughts. How does Ben see the world? As this big, vague distracting thing around the centre of the universe – himself. What is reality to him? Not the forum and medium in which he moves and acts, but a distraction from what he's really doing.

I knew that paying attention to cars when he crosses the street wasn't important to him. And I knew that when his dad or I called him to the table or into the car, the summons always came when he was busy. But I never knew what he thought he was really doing. And now I know. He's thinking.

I think, therefore I am. What a deep kid!

He's thinking about his computer, or frogs, or the ozone layer. He's fixing his skateboard so he can be ready if spring comes in the middle of January. (Not in Northern Alberta, I'm afraid!) He's thinking about whether a *Tyrannosaurus Rex* would be able to reach into his treehouse.

I was understanding my ten-year-old son at last. It felt great. Then he popped back into the kitchen. "Mom?" he said again. "I'm pretty sure I'm going to like girls someday." He popped out and left me there, thinking with an empty teacup.

Parents Don't Want Justice, Parents Want Quiet

It's two days after Christmas. We're all at home, doing about what I'd expected we'd be doing. Bernie is reading the paper, even the want ads after two days of newspaper withdrawal. He's hooked, up to two dailies now, and I think his addiction is getting worse. Both kids are carefully avoiding cleaning their rooms – Lila is playing with her kitten, Ben with his ping-pong set. I am trying to write a couple or three book reviews to sell to magazines so that I can repair the damage to our bank accounts caused by Christmas glee. I'm not having much luck because of Ben's ping-pong game. You see, it's not on a ping-pong table.

I don't know if most people are used to playing table tennis only on a table. By Christmas afternoon my son was re-discovering all kinds of ways of playing with paddles and ping-pong balls, most of which got stopped instantly by his annoyed parents. "No, you can't bounce the ball off the living-room window!" He tried outside, but the wind carried the ball away into the trees. Back inside for another try.

On Boxing Day I heard him talking to himself. "Gotta stay away from windows. Can't knock over the Christmas tree. Too much breakable stuff in the bathroom." He counted his points on his fingers, and suddenly crowed, "I got it!"

He closed the door at the bottom of the stairs, and made his own private racquetball court. The little ball bounces off the walls and stairs, rocketing back and forth with little "tok" sounds that drive my son wild. It drives me crazy, but I try not to let it get to me.

After all, it's noise, but it's play, not fighting. I don't have to break up an argument or referee the game. These are important things for a parent in the first days after Christmas, when Santa has already come and the relatives have left and we're not all on our best behaviour anymore. All I want to do is drink a big mug of tea and get back to my word processor. So if Ben wants to stand at the bottom of the stairs batting ping-pong balls like a wild thing, he's allowed.

He got really inventive yesterday. First he put the kitten at the top of the stairs and tossed the ball up to her. She rolled it around, knocked it downstairs and he hit it back up again. This went on for half an hour till the goggle-eyed kitten staggered off for a nap. Ben wasn't tired yet. He got his sister Lila involved in the game, and it changed again.

They ended up shooting his Nerf Bow-and-Arrow set up and down the stairs, hitting the sponge arrows back with ping-pong paddles. These are supposed to be gifted children, according to the school. Why aren't they off discovering penicillin instead of laughing like maniacs and chanting play-by-play commentary on their sports? What am I supposed to do in all this racket?

It was comedian Bill Cosby who said years ago "Parents don't want Justice, parents want Quiet." And sure, when I'm breaking up an argument, I don't really care so much which kid's fault it is, so long as the fight stops. But maybe this Quest for Quiet isn't my best goal.

I learned to abandon the Quest for Quiet now and then when the twins were small. We'd sing "The Quartermaster's Store" outdoors, really loud, until the neighbours looked out their windows for the "eggs on little tiny legs." We'd be real quiet in art galleries for five minutes, then go out and jump up and down, hooting, on the step. I thought the kids were outgrowing that kind of noise, until a week before Christmas when we were walking to the Library. They walked for a mile, taking turns singing nonsense like "humm-zzingggg" without pause.

Just when I was about to snarl at them to be quiet for a minute, I shut up myself and thought about it. A child babbling nonsense sounds is not whining, complaining or arguing with a sibling. Song games are cooperative, not competitive, and don't need to be picked up when they're done. And just how good can kids be at Christmas time?

So, when a good noise is happening, I have to put the Quest for Quiet on hold for a while. It may mean ping-pong balls bouncing off the wall next to my word processor, but I can cope with the noise while my son works off a little energy. It'll stop as soon as Ben gets working with his Dad on the new Crystal Radio Set, which will happen when Bernie finishes reading the paper. Maybe I should worry about all this newspaper reading – he's up to two papers a day, and it keeps him awfully quiet...

Lost and Found

It should be hard to lose things around my small house on the farm. I can check every cupboard, closet and drawer twice in ten minutes, and still not find what I'm looking for in time for dinner or the schoolbus or anything. When I lose something, I tear from one end of the house to the other as I search, looking under newspapers and emptying the laundry basket.

All it takes to actually find anything I've lost is to ask my husband Bernie where it is. "Where is the school newsletter?" I'll ask, and he'll point to the newsletter stuck to the fridge with a magnet, right where I looked two minutes ago. How does he do it?

"Do we have a Robertson screwdriver?" I'll ask, perched on a kitchen chair to unscrew and move the curtain rods. When I say, "This end is too big," he has the smaller size ready. He keeps his screwdriver set neat in a blue plastic box that doesn't even look like a screwdriver. No wonder I can never find it. Everyone else with screwdrivers in the kitchen puts them handles-up in a coffee can, and you hunt through it for the ones with fancy ends.

Sometimes all I have to do to find things while rummaging is to say out loud to him, "Where the heck is the – oh, there it is." Bernie smugly takes credit for these discoveries.

In fact, Bernie does a lot of things different from everyone else I know. When he does laundry, he folds everything right away when it comes out of the dryer, but he puts all our folded clothes and towels into the baskets all mixed together so we have to hunt for a lost sock or both halves of a gym suit. Bernie insists he never has trouble finding things in the laundry. He even finds and pairs his socks.

This is a real achievement, as socks become truly lost from time to time when they are tumbled in a dryer. Not just lost when I look for them. Not just lost like the sock stuffed up the sleeve of my sweater (which I didn't see till I'd been wearing it around town for hours), or the other sock hanging down from inside the back of that sweater like a tail (which I didn't discover till undressing for bed). There must be some scientific reason for this, maybe something to do with black holes or particle physics. I'll have to ask a scientist about this some day. I even know an astrophysicist – an albino, Australian astrophysicist. Bernie has his address somewhere and I'm sure he could find it if I asked him.

I, however, have trouble even finding Bernie some days. I came indoors one afternoon and caught my daughter looking for the cookie jar. "Where's your dad?" I asked.

She shrugged. "He's probably eating Spaghetti-O's in Montreal." My son didn't know either. He had some experiment going in his room, after finally finding all the bits to one of his sets. Teenagers know parents turn up sooner or later.

I eventually found Bernie hiding on our bed under a mosquito net with the electric fan on high, a magazine and a pint mug of home-mixed Italian Soda with ice. "Shh!" he whispered. "Both kids came home and burst into the kitchen, yelling, 'Taa-Daa!' No reaction. 'Taa-Daa!' louder in the living room, the bathroom, and they eventually gave up yelling and looking for me." He sipped his soda before adding, "I think they found the marshmallows and chocolate chips you were hiding."

"It's not like they really need anymore to find us here when they get home," I pointed out.

"Sooner or later they're gonna look for dinner," he told me. He peered and patted carefully at his blanket. "Where did I put my glasses?" he asked. "Can you find them? I can't put my soda down on the bed! Help! Where the heck are my glasses?"

"Oh, there they are," I crowed. I actually found something for once in my life. I could have run away and hid the glasses, but this time I was the finder. It was my turn to be generous. And come to think of it, it was his turn to go look in the pantry cupboard and find something that looked like dinner.

Don't miss out!

Visit the website below and you can sign up to receive emails whenever Paula Johanson publishes a new book. There's no charge and no obligation.

https://books2read.com/r/B-A-ZKUK-YWJCC

BOOKS 2 READ

Connecting independent readers to independent writers.

Did you love *Working Parent*? Then you should read *Under The Plow*[1] by Paula Johanson!

Under The Plow

BOOK 3 OF SLICE OF LIFE SERIES

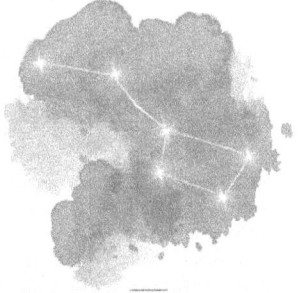

Paula Johanson

[2]

Real life stories can tell who you are, and where you are, and sometimes whether anyone else is like you. Here in *Under the Plow*, there's a lot you'll recognize about home and neighbours or family and gardening, in these real life stories by writer Paula Johanson.

Look here for insights into city folk and country living, as when Paula writes of learning to be both a writer and a farmer, and how can anyone find their way in this part of the world. *"Houses out here don't have numbers by the front doors. Houses out here don't even have stairs by the front door. Some of our neighbours don't even have front doors at all, just a place where a front door will be put some day. Our little white house is the only house out here where the front door gets used. It's the only door we have. But then we're odd. Our neighbours are sure we're odd because we use our front door and didn't use to have a phone."*

---

1. https://books2read.com/u/47VLAR
2. https://books2read.com/u/47VLAR

Under The Plow is a collection of Op-Ed columns written for a weekly rural newspaper in Sturgeon County, Alberta. Doublejoy Books is proud to release this book as the third title in the **Slice of Life** series. As a sequel to *No Parent Is An Island* and *Working Parent*, this book brings the family and writing stories into their prime. If you like the humour and storytelling of Hannah Gadsby, then *Under The Plow* will keep you reading.

"Paula Johanson chronicles the adventure of parenthood with wry wit and ironic accuracy."

- Jim Holland, editor, *Island Parent* magazine

Read more at books2read.com/paulaj.

Also by Paula Johanson

Alt-Academic
Woolgathering: Awareness of the Foreign in Published Works About Cowichan Woolworking
Sanitizer

Prime Ministers of Canada
Pierre Elliott Trudeau: Child of Nature
Charles Tupper: Warhorse

Slice of Life
No Parent Is An Island
Working Parent
Under The Plow

Young Science
Bat Poop Sparkles
Otters Hold Hands

Standalone

Small Rain and Other Nightmares
Island Views
Plum Tree
Tower in the Crooked Wood
King Kwong: Larry Kwong, the China Clipper Who Broke the NHL Colour Barrier
Science Critters
Green Paddler

Watch for more at books2read.com/paulaj.

About the Author

Paula Johanson is a Canadian writer. A graduate of the University of Victoria with an MA in Canadian literature, she has worked as a security guard, a short order cook, a teacher, newspaper writer, and more. As well as editing books and teaching materials, she has run an organic-method small farm with her spouse, raised gifted twins, and cleaned university dormitories. In addition to novels and stories, she is the author of forty-two books written for educational publishers, among them *The Paleolithic Revolution* and *Women Writers* from the series *Defying Convention: Women Who Changed The World*. Johanson is an active member of SF Canada, the national association of science fiction and fantasy authors.

Read more at books2read.com/paulaj.

DOUBLEJOY BOOKS

About the Publisher

Doublejoy Books is the publisher of a variety of eclectic books of Canadian literature.

    http://doublejoybooks.com
    http://books2read.com/paulaj